DISASTERS AND THE ENVIRONMENT

TORNADOES
and the Environment

by Marcia Amidon Lusted

CAPSTONE PRESS
a capstone imprint

Published by Capstone Press, an imprint of Capstone
1710 Roe Crest Drive, North Mankato, Minnesota 56003
capstonepub.com

Copyright © 2026 by Capstone. All rights reserved. No part of this publication may be reproduced in whole or in part, or stored in a retrieval system, or transmitted in any form or by any means, electronic, mechanical, photocopying, recording, or otherwise, without written permission of the publisher.

Library of Congress Cataloging-in-Publication Data is available on the Library of Congress website.
ISBN: 9798875217029 (hardcover)
ISBN: 9798875216978 (paperback)
ISBN: 9798875216985 (ebook PDF)

Summary: Tornadoes can cause a lot of damage to homes and other buildings. They can also damage the environment. Readers will learn how tornadoes affect land and wildlife and how nature can recover from these disasters.

Editorial Credits
Editor: Ashley Kuehl; Designer: Dina Her; Media Researcher: Rebekah Hubstenberger; Production Specialist: Tori Abraham

Image Credits
Alamy: Scott Schilke/Sipa USA, 17; Associated Press: Fred Stewart, 28; Getty Images: Drew Angerer, 26, 29, iStock/EyeEm Mobile GmbH, 7, Joe Raedle, 12, 25, 27, Julie Bennett, 16, Julie Denesha, 19, Kyle Rivas, 22, Mario Tama, 11, Scott Olson, 24, Stocktrek Images, 6, The Boston Globe, 18, Topical Press Agency/Hulton Archive, 13; Shutterstock: artjazz, cover (top), BLAGORODEZ (whirlwind twirl), front and back cover and throughout, Dustie, 15, Jonah Lange, 5, PakulinSergei, 20, Rainer Lesniewski, 9, Tapui, 23, Todd Shoemake, 8, ungvar, 21, VanderWolf Images, 14, Vector_Artist (particle funnel), cover, 1, Wolfilser, cover (bottom)

Any additional websites and resources referenced in this book are not maintained, authorized, or sponsored by Capstone. All product and company names are trademarks™ or registered® trademarks of their respective holders.

Printed and bound in China. 006276

TABLE OF CONTENTS

INTRODUCTION
One Hundred Tornadoes 4

CHAPTER ONE
Where Do Tornadoes Come From? . . 6

CHAPTER TWO
A Path of Destruction 10

CHAPTER THREE
How Do Tornadoes Affect the
Environment? 14

CHAPTER FOUR
After a Tornado 20

CHAPTER FIVE
Humans and Tornadoes 24

Glossary 30
Read More 31
Internet Sites. 31
Index. 32
About the Author 32

Words in **bold** are in the glossary.

Introduction

ONE HUNDRED TORNADOES

It was April 25, 2024. People in the Midwest and Great Plains areas of the United States were used to **severe** weather in the springtime. But the next four days would have many more storms than usual. More than one hundred tornadoes hit the states of Iowa, Kansas, Nebraska, Missouri, Oklahoma, and Texas. Winds blew at speeds of up to 90 miles (145 kilometers) per hour. The winds knocked down power lines and pulled trees from the ground. Some trees landed on buildings and vehicles. The tornadoes destroyed entire towns. Many people lost their homes, businesses, and schools. Farm animals were killed.

What caused so many tornadoes? Cold air in the **atmosphere** met warm, wet air near the ground. Winds changed speed and direction. These conditions caused strong storms. Heavy rain and large chunks of hail fell and caused flooding. These storms also caused tornadoes.

A tornado passes over Minden, Iowa, on April 26, 2024.

Chapter One

WHERE DO TORNADOES COME FROM?

A tornado is a column of air that spins up to 250 miles (402 km) per hour. Tornadoes are caused by thunderstorms called supercell thunderstorms. They are gigantic and last a long time.

A satellite view shows a storm just before it formed a tornado that hit Moore, Oklahoma, in 2013.

A supercell storm cloud spins over Malta, Montana.

Thunderstorms happen when cold, dry air moves over warm, humid air. The warm air then pushes up through the cold air. That's called an updraft. If the thunderstorm's winds change speed or direction, the updraft begins to rotate, or turn. It rotates faster and faster until a **funnel cloud** forms. The funnel cloud reaches down to the ground. It is now a tornado.

FACT

Tornadoes most often occur during the afternoon and evening. By then, the sun has been heating the atmosphere all day.

The United States has more tornadoes than any other country. After the United States, Bangladesh and Argentina have tornadoes most often. But nearly all continents have some tornadoes.

A storm with hail and a tornado sweeps through the border between Colorado and Oklahoma.

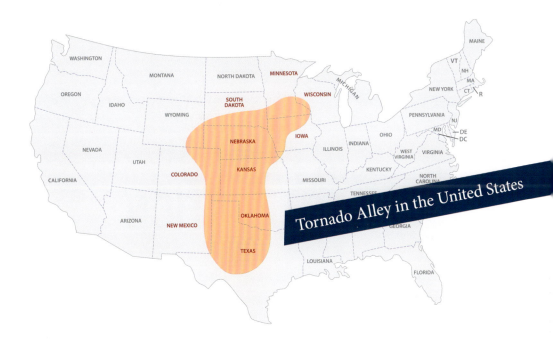

Tornado Alley in the United States

The United States gets more of these storms because no other place has the same **climates** arranged in the same way. The U.S. has warm, moist air from the Gulf of Mexico in the south. This meets cool, dry air from the Rocky Mountains in the north. Dry air also comes from the deserts in the southwest. In the middle states, these two types of air meet. These states are most likely to get tornadoes.

FACT

Tornado Alley gets the most tornadoes in the country. This area includes Iowa, Nebraska, Texas, Kansas, South Dakota, and Oklahoma.

Chapter Two

A PATH OF DESTRUCTION

Tornadoes are destructive. The Enhanced Fujita Scale, or EF Scale, measures a tornado by how much damage it does. The damage tells scientists how fast the winds were.

An EF0 tornado causes almost no damage. An EF1 can tip over mobile homes and break windows. An EF2 destroys mobile homes, snaps trees, and damages roofs. An EF3 rips roofs and walls from buildings and uproots most trees. In an EF4, most buildings are destroyed. Cars fly through the air. An EF5 lifts and blows away houses. Concrete buildings are damaged. The bark blows off trees.

EF Scale

Tornado Rating	Wind Speed in Miles per Hour
EF0	65 to 85 (105 to 137 km)
EF1	86 to 110 (138 to 177 km)
EF2	111 to 135 (179 to 217 km)
EF3	136 to 165 (219 to 266 km)
EF4	166 to 200 (267 to 322 km)
EF5	above 200 (322 km)

The town of Joplin, Missouri, had severe damage after being hit by an EF5 tornado in May 2011.

Every year, tornadoes kill about 70 people. They also cause about $400 million in damage. Strong winds blow away mobile homes, sheds, and vehicles. Buildings lose their roofs and sometimes collapse. The wind can drive splinters of wood into tree trunks and walls. Shingles, broken glass, doors, and metal rods become dangerous missiles.

Tornado winds blew splintered tree branches into a car in Joplin, Missouri, in 2011.

Case Study
1925 Tri-State Tornado

The deadliest tornado in U.S. history happened on March 18, 1925. It had wind speeds of more than 300 miles (483 km) per hour. The tornado stayed on the ground for three and a half hours. It moved through Missouri, Illinois, and Indiana. Six hundred ninety-five people died. Sixty-nine of them were children at school. The Tri-State Tornado destroyed 15,000 homes. Recovery help came from the Red Cross. Relief trains took injured people to hospitals. The National Guard helped rebuild destroyed towns, and people donated supplies and equipment. But it still took months to rebuild.

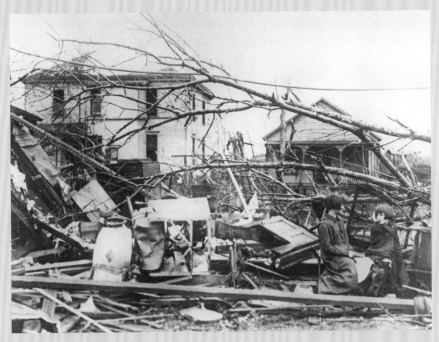

Chapter Three

HOW DO TORNADOES AFFECT THE ENVIRONMENT?

Tornadoes also damage the environment. During the April 2024 tornadoes in the Great Plains and Midwest, wind ripped tree roots out of the ground. Trees can also fall over or break. Branches fall off and trunks can be twisted. Later, piles of dead trees can become fuel for wildfires.

FACT

Can a tornado really pick up a cow? People in Elgin, Texas, say that it can. Witnesses reported seeing a 2017 tornado toss three cows over a fence into another field.

An EF5 tornado left these trees without leaves or branches.

The thunderstorms that form the tornado bring heavy rain. In July 2010, rainstorms that happened along with 10 tornadoes in Wisconsin caused multiple rivers to flood.

Flooding can create pools of water that can take oxygen and **nutrients** out of the soil. This harms or kills plants and trees. Chemicals may leak after damage to farm or factory buildings. This can **pollute** rivers, lakes, and groundwater.

Tornadoes also affect animals. Flooding can change the flow of water in streams. This **disrupts** the **habitat** of animals that live there. High winds destroy bird nests. Wind can blow **debris** such as branches and shredded bark. They cover the entrances to burrows. Animals may have trouble finding food.

A group of tornadoes caused flooding in Ohatchee, Alabama, in March 2021.

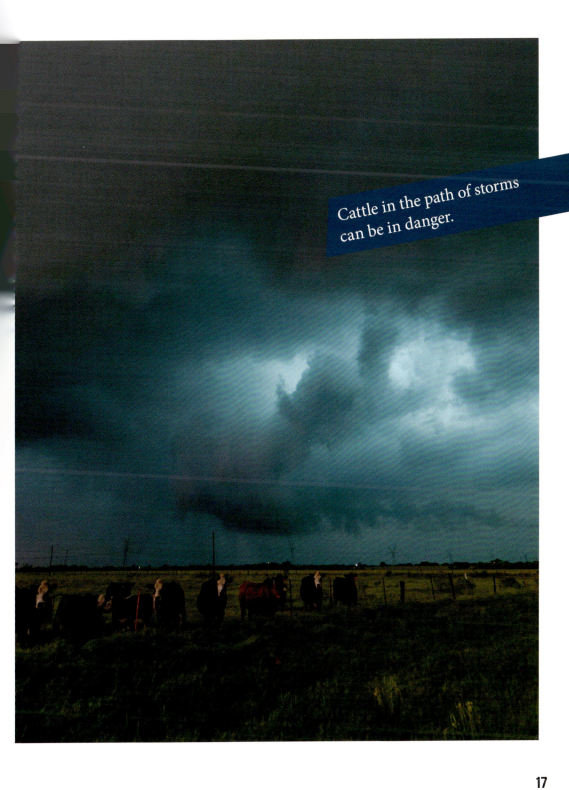
Cattle in the path of storms can be in danger.

Case Study

Worcester Tornado

A strong tornado hit the city of Worcester, Massachusetts, on June 9, 1953. Winds were more than 300 miles (483 km) per hour. Hailstones the size of baseballs fell. The tornado traveled 45 miles (72 km). It was 1 mile (1.6 km) wide by the time it reached Worcester. Witnesses saw three tornado funnels on the ground at the same time. Ninety-four people died, and 10,000 people lost their homes. Strong winds lifted houses and dropped them in a nearby lake. Trees broke and flew through the air. Debris flew up to 75 miles (121 km) away. Some even landed in the Atlantic Ocean.

After the storm, people came together to help. They cleared away debris, but some things stayed where they landed in lakes and the ocean. Businesses refused to charge people who were buying supplies. People all over the country donated money. All that help let Worcester rebuild quickly.

A robin sings in a tree after tornadoes tore off leaves and branches.

Animals can be killed during a tornado. Birds that get caught in the storm's winds may die. Strong winds can pick up and drop animals. Falling trees can hit animals. Some may drown in floods.

Chapter Four

AFTER A TORNADO

Even when a tornado is over, conditions can be dangerous. The wires of blown-down electrical lines are dangerous. Leaking gas lines are a fire hazard with a risk of explosions. Water and **sewage** systems can be damaged. Buildings may be unsafe.

Leaked oil pollutes a pond, turning the water rainbow colors.

After a big storm, broken power lines and systems can be dangerous.

The environment can be damaged too. Strong winds can blow away soil and plants. Tornadoes lift pollutants into the air. This can include smoke, dust, and chemicals, which are unhealthy for people and animals. **Hazardous** materials may leak from damaged buildings. Oil, chemicals, and sewage can pollute soil and water. These pollutants can kill plants. Animals that drink the water may get sick or die.

Tornadoes leave animals injured and frightened. Debris can hit wild animals, farm animals, and pets. They may try to run away. People's pets may get lost after their homes are damaged or destroyed. They may not be able to find food or water. Some animals get trapped in buildings or piles of debris.

People work to free a horse that flew through the air and got stuck in a pool of water during a 2019 tornado in Kansas.

Children can help after a storm by planting trees.

Wild animals might look for new places to live. This can put them in conflict with humans and pets. If animals' usual food sources are destroyed, they may need to look for food. Not having food or water can cause stress for these creatures. Tornadoes can damage or destroy the biodiversity, or different kinds of plants and animals, of an area.

It takes time for the environment to recover after a tornado. Small, quick-growing plants come first. Later on, bigger bushes and trees grow. People can help by planting trees in damaged areas. Cleaning up polluted areas can help too.

Chapter Five

HUMANS AND TORNADOES

People and communities suffer when tornadoes happen. Some people may be injured or even die. People may not have anywhere to live. Stores, churches, and businesses may be damaged or gone. People lose the things that make their town a community. It may take time to rebuild. In the meantime, people may not be able to go to work and school.

People clean up damage after a 2004 tornado in Utica, Illinois.

A resident of Joplin, Missouri, works to rebuild his house after a 2012 tornado.

As well as being affected by tornadoes, humans may affect storm patterns. Human actions are causing climate change to happen faster. Burning fossil fuels such as coal, oil, and natural gas releases carbon into the atmosphere. Carbon traps heat. The heat causes more severe storms to happen.

Tornadoes need warm, wet air. But they also need changes in wind direction. Scientists have discovered that changes in wind direction are actually slowing down. This might mean that fewer tornadoes will happen. Scientists aren't sure yet if climate change will change how often tornadoes happen.

The Doppler on Wheels can drive into big storms to gather scientific data.

FACT

Scientists aren't sure if the number of tornadoes is increasing or if new technology is just better at recording them.

Tornadoes happen around the world. The best thing to do is to be prepared. People should check local weather forecasts. They should have a plan for the safest place to go if a tornado comes. This can be an inside room or a basement. It could also mean lying down in a ditch outside. Communities may have warning sirens. When people hear them, everyone needs to find shelter.

A tornado shelter in Joplin, Missouri

Case Study
1974 Super Outbreak

The Super Outbreak happened on April 3 and 4 of 1974. These tornadoes in the Midwest and South killed 335 people. It was the first time that more than 100 tornadoes formed in just 24 hours. The Red Cross came. The Army brought in experts to help with rebuilding. President Richard Nixon visited and later signed a bill to give people more help after tornadoes. After the Super Outbreak, many towns and cities installed tornado sirens to warn people about storms. Scientists also began working on new kinds of radar and other technologies.

A weather scientist tracks a storm as part of a tornado research project.

Scientists continue to study tornado patterns and how they affect the environment. They are developing new ways to **predict** tornadoes. New technology can scan an entire storm in just one minute. Forecasters see tornadoes forming. New kinds of radar that use **artificial intelligence** can warn people much faster than before. They hope that being better prepared will mean tornadoes cause less damage to people and the environment.

Glossary

artificial intelligence (ahr-tuh-FISH-uhl in-TEL-ih-juhns)—computer systems that have been trained to do things humans can do, such as understand and produce language

atmosphere (AT-muhs-feer)—the layer of gases that surround Earth

climate (KLYE-mit)—the average weather conditions in a place

debris (duh-BREE)—scattered pieces left after something has been destroyed

disrupt (dis-RUHPT)—to interrupt something so that it cannot continue in the same way

funnel cloud (FUHN-uhl KLOUD)—a cone- or needle-shaped cloud that extends down from a bigger cloud

habitat (HAB-i-tat)—the place where a plant or animal naturally lives and grows

hazardous (HAZ-ur-duhs)—causing a danger or risk

nutrient (NOO-tree-uhnt)—a substance needed by a living thing to stay healthy

pollute (puh-LOOT)—to introduce harmful materials into the environment

predict (pri-DIKT)—to say what you think will happen in the future

severe (suh-VEER)—causing great damage or difficulty

sewage (SOO-ij)—waste matter such as feces or dirty water from homes and factories

Read More

Abramson, Marcia. *Tornadoes*. Minneapolis: Bearport Publishing, 2024.

Corrigan, Kathleen. *Tornadoes: Causes and Effects.* Mankato, MN: 12-Story Library, 2022.

Crane, Cody. *All About Tornadoes*. New York: Children's Press, 2022.

Internet Sites

National Geographic Kids: Tornadoes
kids.nationalgeographic.com/science/article/tornado

SciJinks: What Causes Tornadoes?
scijinks.gov/tornado

Weather WizKids: Tornadoes
weatherwizkids.com/weather-tornado.htm

Index

animals, 4, 14, 16, 17, 19, 21, 22, 23

climate change, 25, 26

electrical lines, 20, 21
Enhanced Fujita Scale, 10, 11

flooding, 5, 15, 16, 19
forecasts, 27
funnel clouds, 7

gas lines, 20

pollutants, 21, 23
preparation for tornadoes, 27, 29

scientists, 10, 26, 28, 29
soil, 15, 21
Super Outbreak, 28

Tornado Alley, 9
trees, 4, 10, 12, 14, 15, 19, 23
Tri-State Tornado, 13

updrafts, 7

wind direction changes, 5, 26

About the Author

Marcia Amidon Lusted has written 200 books and more than 600 articles for young readers of all ages. She is the former editor of *AppleSeeds* magazine for children. She also writes and edits for adults, as well as working in sustainable development. You can see more about her books at www.adventuresinnonfiction.com.